Starter Book B

Words at Work ✓

Word-level and Sentence-level Work for Excellence in Spelling and Grammar

JO PHENIX

First published in the United Kingdom in 2000 by

Folens Publishers
Albert House
Apex Business Centre
Boscombe Road
Dunstable
Bedfordshire
LU5 4RL

Jo Phenix hereby asserts her moral right to be identified as the author of this work in accordance with the Copyright, Designs and Patents Act 1988. Additional material by Mary Green.

Editor: Jennifer Steele
Layout artist: James Brown
Illustrations: Sue Woollatt (Graham-Cameron Illustration)
Brian Lee (Graham-Cameron Illustration)
Cover artist: Jock MacRae
Page design: Turners Creative
Cover design: Martin Cross

British Library Cataloguing in Publication Data.
A catalogue record for this book is available from the British Library.
Printed in China through World Print.
ISBN 1 84163 387-9

Words at Work ✓

Contents

Building Words

Working With Words and Sentences

Shopping Spree

Here are the **consonants**:

b c d f g h j
k l m n p q r
s t v w
x y z

A Jane and Giles can only buy foods that begin with a consonant. Help them to choose the correct foods.

Write the foods that Jane and Giles can buy:

1. tomato
2. ______
3. ______
4. ______
5. ______
6. ______
7. ______

Playing in the Park

Listen to the sounds at the beginning, middle and end of words.

A Fill in the missing letters to name things that you can see in this park. They have all been left white.

1. ca p

2. ___ ree

3. ___ alloons

4. sand ___ i ___

5. boa ___

6. ___ ite

7. do ___

8. ne ___

9. ___ utterfly.

B Now colour in all the things that you have named.

Double Letters

Sometimes **consonants** can be **double letters** in the middle of words.

A Say the name of each picture. Listen for the sound in the middle of the words. Write the missing letters for each word. Use two of the same letters each time.

1. bu f f alo

2. ra ____ ____ it

3. ki ____ ____ en

4. cli ____ ____ ers

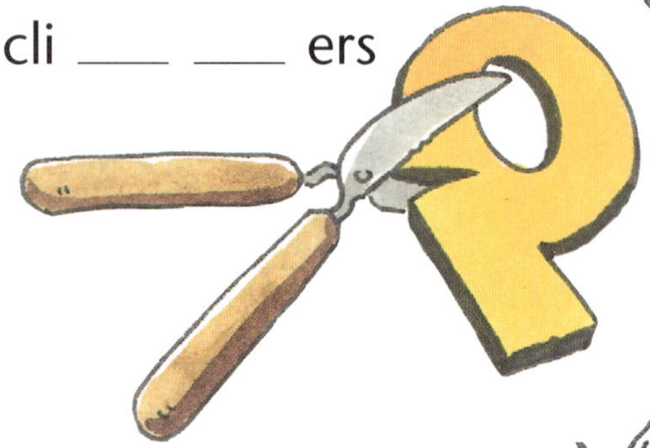

5. ha ____ ____ er

6. la____ ____ er

Word Sums

Sometimes **consonants** can work together at the beginning of words, such as **sw**, **bl**, **cr**, **tr**, and **str**.

A Do the word sums like this and say the words:

sw + eet = sweet.

bl + ow = blow

bl + ack = ____________

cr + ab = ____________

cr + oss = ____________

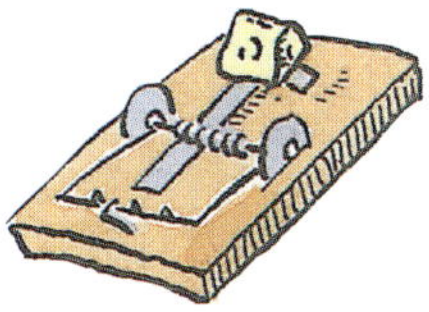

tr + ap = ____________

tr + ip = ____________

B Now try these word sums and say the words.

str + ing = ____________

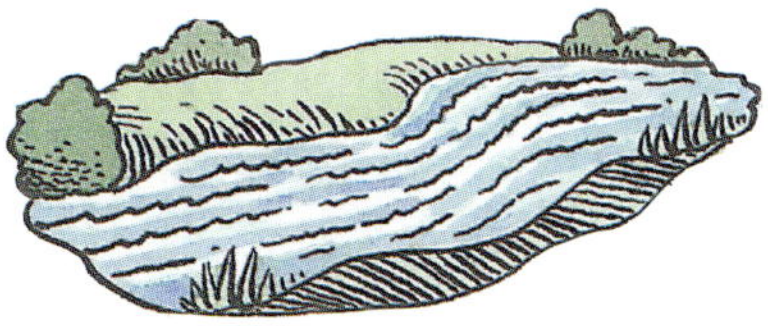

str + eam = ____________

C Choose the right words from the words above and put them in the spaces below. Read the sentences.

I have shiny ____________ hair.

I saw a tiny ____________ on the sand.

Thread the beads on the ____________ .

Help!

Sometimes two **consonants** can work together at the end of words, such as **lp**, **ld**, **st**.

A Put **lp** in the words and say them:

he ______ ye ______ .

- Read these sentences:

"Help!" shouted the man with the bee on his nose.

"Yelp!" said the dog with the cut on his paw.

B Put **ld** in the words and say them:

he ______ co ______ .

- Put the words in the right spaces:

I ______ out my hand for my Mum to put a plaster on it.

I was so ______ I could not keep still.

C Put **st** in the words and say them:

pe ______ ea ______ we ______

- Put the words in the right spaces:

"Tidy your room, you little ______!" said my Mum.

North, south, ______ and ______ .

Sound Spells

The **vowels** are:

a e i o u.

Remember that every word must have a vowel.

A Wanda Witch is making words. How many words can you make using the letters in her spell jars? You can use each letter more than once.

cat

span

The Moon Is Made of Cheese

Sometimes two **vowels** can work together to make one sound.

A Write the **oo** words in the moon. Write the **ee** words in the cheese.

tree	boot	weed	food
zoo	roof	green	jeep
look	stool	bees	sleep

cheese

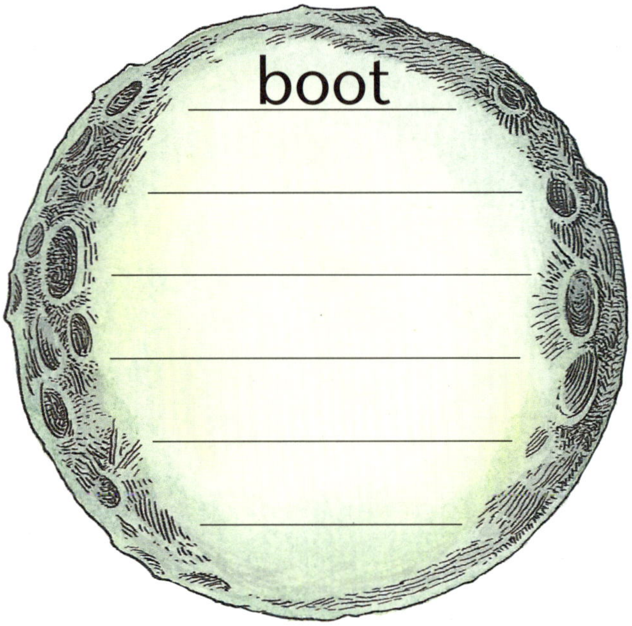

moon

B Read this rhyme:

The sun is just a grapefruit,
The sky is honey from the bees,
The stars are little beetroots,
The moon is made of cheese.

Mary Green.

- Underline the **ee** and **oo** words.

A Rainy Day Means No Play!

A Write the **ai** sounds in the words. Say the words.

r_a_ _i_n s___ ___l t___ ___l ch___ ___n tr___ ___n

B Read these sentences:

On Monday there was rain and hail so we had no playtime.

On Tuesday my friend painted a picture of a green mountain.

- Underline all the **ai** sounds.

C Finish these sentences:

On Wednesday I ______________________________.

On Thursday my teacher ______________________________.

On Friday my class ______________________________.

On Saturday ______________________________.

On Sunday ______________________________.

- Underline all the **ay** sounds.

Which One?

A Ring the word that fits the picture.

my (boat) goat

by soap road

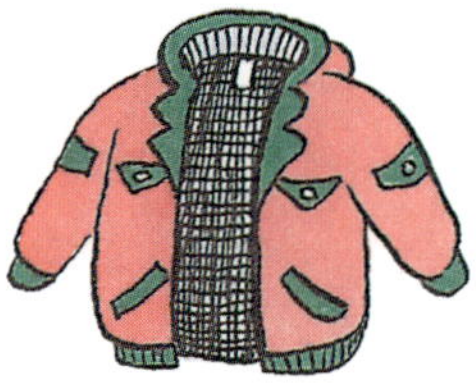

oak fly coat

coach tie roast

lie cloak toad

loaf foal fry

cry throat coast

croak try stoat

pie float oats

B Choose the right word from the words above and write them in the spaces.

We went on a c<u>oach</u> to the seaside. There were lots of cars on the r________ and it took a long time to get there. I felt sleepy and had to l________ down on the seat. When we came to the c________ I woke up. We had apple p________ and ice cream and sailed on a b________.

Drum Beat

Words have beats or **syllables**. For example, *cat* has one beat, *kitten* has two – *kit-ten*. Tap out the beat in the words.

A Willie Wise's One Man Band has come to town! How many syllables are there in the names of each of the instruments that he is playing? Write the numbers next to each instrument.

1. drum 1

2. guitar ______

3. trumpet ______

4. banjo ______

5. cymbal ______

6. bell ______

7. flute ______

8. triangle ______

Play Time

Words have beats or **syllables**.

A Saleema likes to do things with two syllables. In the spaces below write the activities with two syllables to find out what she likes to do.

1. football
2. ____________
3. ____________
4. ____________
5. ____________
6. ____________
7. ____________

Syllable Circus

Words have beats or **syllables**.

A Count the number of syllables in each circus word. Write the words in the correct list.

Circus words

band	monkey	acrobat	tiger	juggler
elephant	puppet	clown	horse	lion

one syllable	two syllables	three syllables
1. band	1. monkey	1. acrobat
2. ______	2. ______	2. ______
3. ______	3. ______	
	4. ______	
	5. ______	

Two Words Together

Sometimes two words join together to make a **compound word**.

A Look at the pictures below. Add them to the words to make compound words. For example, *snow + man = snowman.*

snow + 

snow man

snow ______

rain + 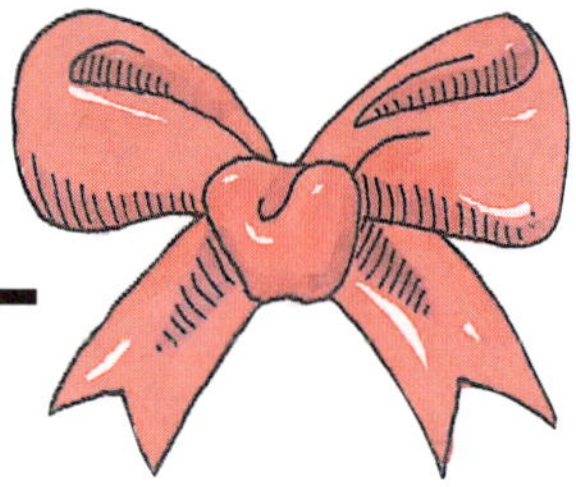

rain ______

rain ______

sun + 

sun ______

sun ______

foot + 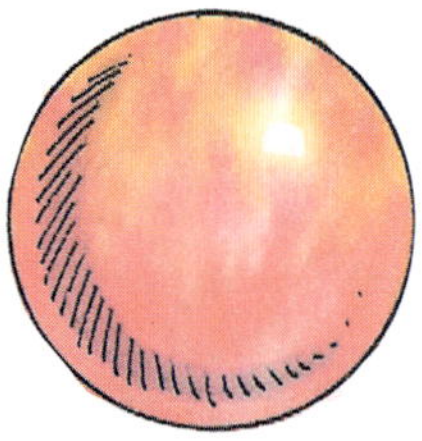

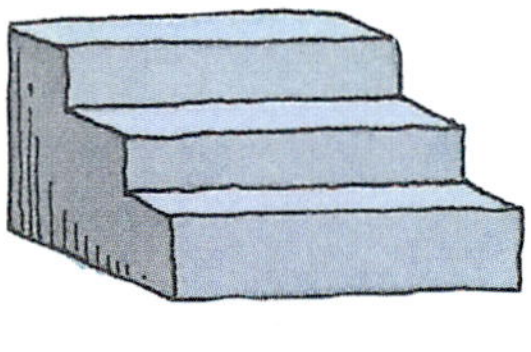

foot ______

foot ______

Rebus Addition

Sometimes two words join together to make a **compound word**.

A Can you solve these picture clues? Say the name of each picture. Write the words to make compound words.

 +  = pineapple

 +  = ____________

\+  = ____________

 +  = ____________

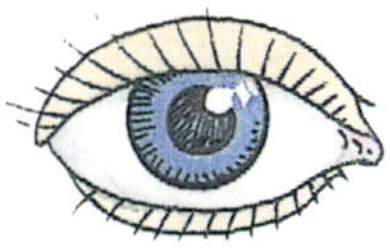 +  = ____________

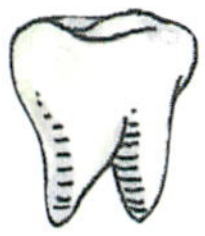 +  = ____________

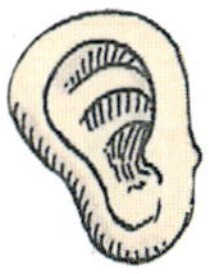 +  = ____________

Party List

When a word means that there is *more than one* it is a **plural** word.

A Help Katie to plan her party. Choose ten things from the list in the box. Write them in the plural on your shopping list. Remember to add an **s** to each word.

party words

balloon	cake	present	game
spoon	card	fork	cup
stamp	drink	plate	bowl

What Do You Need?

When a word means that there is *more than one* it is a **plural** word.

A Look at the pictures below. How many of each thing do you need? The words are around the pictures. Remember that you only need to add an **s** if the word means more than one.

To play catch:

one ball ____________

two ____________

two ____________

two ____________

To go sledging:

one jacket ____________

one ____________

one ____________

two ____________

two ____________

Let's Count

When a word means that there is *more than one* it is a **plural** word.

A Look at the things in the picture. Count them and complete the sentences. Remember to add an **s** to your words.

Word box

book	table	picture	chair
apple	cat	toy	

1. There are two t a b l e s .
2. There are three c ___ ___ ___ .
3. There are four c ___ ___ ___ ___ ___ .
4. There are five t ___ ___ ___ .
5. There are six p ___ ___ ___ ___ ___ ___ ___ .
6. There are seven a ___ ___ ___ ___ ___ .
7. There are eight b ___ ___ ___ ___ .

B Now colour in the picture.

All Ready!

A Look at the pictures. Sally and Tom are going on holiday. Put **ed** in the spaces and read the sentences.

1. Sally pack<u>ed</u> her bags.

2. Tom open_____ the boot.

3. Dave fold_____ the tent.

4. Patch jump_____ on the seat.

5. Gran lock_____ the door.

6. Mum start_____ the car.

Going Camping

A Look at the pictures. What is the family doing?
Put **ing** in the spaces and read the sentences.

1. Tom is lick ing a lolly.

2. Dave is cook______ some food.

3. Mum is read______ a book.

4. Gran is kick______ a ball.

5. Sally is swing______ on a tree.

6. Patch is chew______ a bone.

Dressing-Up Colours

These are **colour words**: *black, white, grey, blue, red, yellow, green, orange, purple* and *brown.*

A Tamara, Josh and Amber are dressing up in some old clothes. Fill in the sentences below to say what colours each of them is wearing.

1. Tamara is wearing a ____red____ hat, an ____________ scarf and a ____________ dress.

2. Josh is wearing a ____________ hat, a ____________ jacket, ____________ trousers and ____________ socks.

3. Amber is wearing a ____________ hat, a ____________ blouse and a ____________ skirt.

Family Diary

These are the **days of the week**: *Monday, Tuesday, Wednesday, Thursday, Friday, Saturday* and *Sunday.*

A Help Kim to write about what she and her sister Kayleigh did with their family on their half-term holiday. Fill in the days of the week in order, starting with Monday.

1. On Monday
my sister and I went shopping with Mum.

2. On ____________
Grandad took us to the circus.

3. On ____________
we played with cousin Karen and her brother.

4. On ____________
Aunt Simone and Uncle Bob visited us.

5. On ____________
we had tea with Gran.

6. On ____________
we played with Dad.

7. On ____________
the family had a party!

B Now underline all the family words that you can find. For example, *sister* is a family word.

What's Happening?

Sentences start with a **capital letter**.

A Write a sentence about each picture. Remember to begin each sentence with a capital letter and end it with a full stop.

Invitations

Special names, days of the week and the names of the months should all begin with **capital letters**.

A The computer did not print the capital letters on some of the special names below. Put a line through the letters that should be capitals.

Start With a Capital

Titles start with **capital letters**.

A Write the titles of these films. Start the words with capital letters.

1. Three Bad Eggs

2. ______________________

3. ______________________

4. ______________________

5. ______________________

6. ______________________

B Which film would you go to see? Finish the sentence.

I would see ______________________________ .

That's the End

Sentences start with a **capital letter** and end with a **full stop**.

A Carlos is writing his diary. The capital letters and full stops are missing from his sentences. Circle the letters that should be capital letters and add the full stops at the ends of the sentences.

Dear Diary,

i had fun today. amy and i took a sledge to the park we rode down the hill i fell off three times we made a snowman we gave him a carrot nose amy put her hat on his head it was a fun day

B Now write two sentences about what you did yesterday.

What Did You Say?

Some **sentences** ask a **question**. They always end with a **question mark**. A question mark looks like this: **?**

A These are question words: *who, where, what, why, when*. This is a question: *Where are you?* Look at the pictures below. Write underneath each picture what question you think is being asked.

1. ______________________________

____

2. ______________________________

____

3. ______________________________

____

4. ______________________________

____

Sentence Scramble

A What are these nursery rhyme characters saying? To find out, unscramble the **sentences** and write them under each picture.

my sheep I've lost

____

______________________________ .

spiders scared I'm of

____

______________________________ .

down fall this time
Don't

____

______________________________ .

fall I hope don't off
this wall I

____

______________________________ .

Winter Wonderland

Sentences start with a **capital letter** and end with a **full stop**.

A Choose a person or thing from the snowflake. Choose a matching event from the snowball. Put them together to make four sentences about winter.

1. ______________________________

2. ______________________________

3. ______________________________

4. ______________________________

B Now write a sentence of your own about winter.

____

____

Timetable

Sentences start with a **capital letter** and end with a **full stop**.

A What did you do at school yesterday? Write one sentence after each heading saying what you did before school, in the morning, in the afternoon and after school.

Date ______________________________

Before school ______________________________

____

Morning ______________________________

____

Afternoon ______________________________

____

After school ______________________________

____

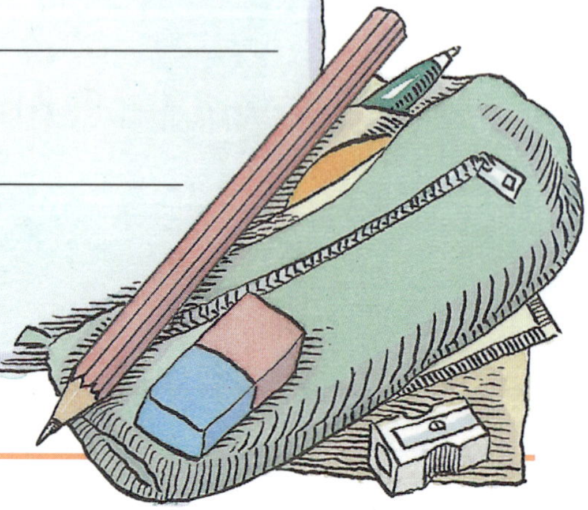